pavlova

by Genevieve Knights

www.pavlovabook.com

Contents

About the Author

Genevieve Knights is a chef, food writer and food photographer based in Auckland, New Zealand. In her early twenties, she took on her first executive chef role at a small café, before honing her skills for the popular restaurant chain GPK, and her culinary career now spans two decades. From the beginning, Genevieve's motto has been to gain the best experience possible by working for those at the top of their game – including iconic hospitality establishments like The French Café, Wheeler's Restaurant and Mantells of Mount Eden.

Over the years, Genevieve also discovered a passion for recipe writing and her work has been published in *Cuisine*, *Foodtown Magazine* and *New Zealand Golf Magazine* among others. The website "Genevieve's Cuisine" went online in 2004 followed shortly after by her first book, *Basic But Brilliant*, in 2005. In creating the website and her three cookbooks, Genevieve has also diversified into food photography and continues to write and photograph recipes promoting quality branded products.

She lives with her husband and business partner Wayne Knights in the suburb of Parnell in Auckland's central business district. Their first joint project, *scones*, was published under the White Knights banner in New Zealand in early 2010, and released in Europe by Welsh publisher Accent Press later in the year. *pavlova* is the second title in their innovative yet accessible series of baking books.

Pavlova History

Anna Pavlova (1885–1931) was an internationally renowned Russian ballerina who travelled the world performing for fascinated audiences in what must have been, for many, their first glimpse of top-class ballet. Some of her dancing can even be viewed online at YouTube in old black-and-white film without sound. It strikes me as a very different form of ballet to that we know today as she never turned out her hands and feet. However, while she was not considered a great beauty, it is said that when she began to dance you simply could not pull your eyes away from her magnetic performance.

A visit to New Zealand in 1926 made a very large impact on those who saw Pavlova dance and much was done in order to impress her. It was known that she was fond of meringues, and according to one tale a Wellington chef may have created the first pavlova cake in her honour and served it to her in the year of her tour. Sadly, there is no way to verify this story. Nevertheless, *The Pavlova Story* by anthropologist Helen Leach published by Otago University Press in 2008 sheds new light on the history of this country's national dessert and how it came to be named.

It was fashionable around this time to develop cakes and desserts and name them in someone's honour – "Peach Melba", named after Australian operatic soprano Dame Nellie Melba (1861–1931) is one that often springs to mind. The earliest recorded recipe for a meringue sweet to be called "Pavlova" was published in New Zealand in 1928. Created by Dunedin home cook Rose H. Rutherford and published by Christchurch's *Weekly Press* under the name "Pavlova Cakes", these were small, piped, coffee essence and walnut meringues. Apart from the coffee meringues, another dish named after the acclaimed ballerina was a four-layer moulded jello, but it was the cake that held on to the name.

Under the pseudonym "Festival", a recipe for the first "Pavlova Cake" as we know it today was published in the *N.Z. Dairy Exporter Annual* in 1929 in a brief description of two short sentences. As was typical of the time, recipes by home cooks assumed a certain amount of cooking knowledge on the part of the reader. It was made up of sugar, egg whites and cornflour, with no vinegar, separated into two and baked in sandwich tins. A single-layer cake also going under the name "Pavlova Cake" appeared in the *Rangiora Mother's Union Cookery Book of Tried and Tested Recipes* in 1933, courtesy of local woman

Laurina Stevens. This two egg white "pav" was also baked in a sandwich tin, and once again with cornflour but no vinegar.

A pavlova made with vinegar appeared in 1934 in the newly launched *New Zealand Woman's Weekly*, when a reader wrote in asking for a reliable pavlova recipe. Another reader responded under the name of "Successful Pavlova-Maker" with a recipe containing four egg whites, one breakfast cup of sugar and one teaspoon of vinegar to be cooked in a round cake tin. Whereas both Rutherford's and "Festival's" recipes called for a very slow oven, cooking instructions around this time first began to advise placing the pav in a hot oven then turning down the heat.

What is clear is that recipes for the meringue cake began to circulate in New Zealand in the late 1920s. In 1929 the name started changing from meringue cake to pavlova and was printed as such in a number of publications by 1934. Also in 1934, a recipe which appeared in the Wellington YMCA fundraising *Blue Triangle Cookery Book* called for the pavlova cake to be baked directly on top of greased paper instead of in a sandwich tin. All the cakes mentioned garnishing with whipped cream and other toppings like nuts and fruit.

Meanwhile, on the other side of the Tasman, Bert Sasche was credited with inventing the Australian pavlova cake in 1935, although there is currently no record of a pavlova recipe published in Australia prior to 1940. The pavlova roll, on the other hand, did indeed emerge from Australia in the 1970s and was later adopted by New Zealand around 1980. (Although, for the life of me, I still cannot fathom why this recipe was spread thin, baked and then rolled up when it cooks beautifully into the shape of a pavlova cake and in a fraction of the time – of course, it lacks the crisp exterior, but to me that just opens it up to all new possibilities as you will see in the "Innovative Pavlova" chapter of this book.)

Meringue cakes, however, were by no means exclusive to Australia and New Zealand. Variations were circulated in newspapers and magazines around the western world in the 1920s and even a little earlier. They were close relatives of crisp meringue layered tortes of the kind made in Europe for centuries and some even had vinegar in the ingredients. So, given that most new recipes are modified from existing ones, instead of speculating endlessly about who first invented the pavlova, the more relevant question might be: *When did the name change from meringue cake to pavlova?*

Pavlova might now be considered an "old-fashioned" dessert, but perhaps it is we that have let the recipe down. When did we stop trying to come up with new variations and why? Maybe it is time to breathe some life back into this long-adored recipe inseparable from our childhoods growing up as barefoot, freckled, beach-loving kids and do our part to ensure it is likewise cemented into the hearts of future generations.

Pavlova Secrets

It was with no little fear and serious self-doubt that I launched into writing a book about a classic and much-loved recipe known mostly unflavoured and baked in three forms – cake, roll, and sometimes miniature. But it was the crazed looks others gave me on mentioning the subject that steeled my resolve to conquer such an unforgiving recipe. "You can't possibly come up with 50 pavlova recipes," everyone insisted. "Watch me!" I replied, yet always thinking in the back of my mind – *What have I gotten myself into?*

From its modest coffee meringue beginning through to its classic four egg white cake manifestation, I was aware that the pavlova recipe was a tried and true icon of Australasian culinary culture. A genuine phoenix rising from the ashes, these were cakes that had been tested and refined for generations by many a keen home cook eager to impress their guests. Of course, if the recipe was easy, what would there be to impress those guests with?

Very quickly I discovered that, though my ideas were many, there is not all that much room to move within the recipe. You always encounter some obstacles in recipe writing but this was ridiculous! Eventually I found ways around the impasse as I grew more familiar with the scientific *rules*, but still I find it curious how other food writers have tackled the recipe in the past.

For instance, I have seen perfect-looking photographs of pavlova but the recipe mentions folding through chopped chocolate. Pavlova is essentially foam and loses volume when it comes into contact with fats and oil. This means everything from egg yolk to chocolate to ground nuts will make the mixture flop leaving you with a large crater in your one-centimetre-high pav. Or snowy-white pavlova without cracks in magazines – now I could smell a slow, dried meringue rat! No wonder this was a recipe to confound the home cooks who, no matter what they tried, could never obtain a result that looked like the recipe photo.

Personally, I love pavlova! It was always my birthday cake of choice as a child and still is to this day. (Thanks, Mum!) I love the soft marshmallow inside, the crunchy cracked exterior, and I don't give a damn if it sinks slightly in the middle. It is what it is. So my goal instead is to celebrate the cake the way it is meant to be yet present new ways of serving it that you may never have imagined. My dearest hope, though, is that you can put aside all the advice you may have heard previously and keep an open mind when reading my tips. Having made over 300 pavlovas in the creation of this book, I have learned some tricks that I want to share, even though I know reading them may not ring the right bell with what a dear relative may or may not have told you in the past.

Now to dispel those myths!

Equipment

It is true that all your equipment should be very clean. The old maxim of rubbing everything with lemon juice then drying it was a way to remove any excess grease that might endanger the foam. You can still do this if you choose, but these days dishwashers do such a good job of removing grease that, if you have a good machine, I shouldn't bother with the lemon juice.

Electric mixers do make a good pavlova but some caution needs to be taken to avoid over-whipping. An over-whipped pavlova develops a honeycomb-style cracked pattern on the surface. Please read the whisking section below for more information. Hand beaters are also okay but it is hard work and may take longer to get the desired result. All the recipes in this book were tested with a hand-held electric beater for the sake of consistency.

Use a large stainless steel bowl if possible. Plastic bowls can carry flavours and grease from other food, glass is heavy to work with, and aluminium is a no-no due to the folding in of vinegar or other acids.

Egg whites

There are so many stories about eggs – use old eggs, use fresh eggs, use room-temperature eggs, use chilled eggs. My results were consistent whether using egg whites that were chilled or room temperature. Fresh and a couple of weeks old were all fine, but if that egg floats in water, don't use it for anything, throw it away.

I found that egg whites that had been separated from yolks a week prior worked but not two weeks prior. Thawed frozen egg whites can take on extra moisture and be unreliable so are best not to use up on special occasions.

All recipes were tested with large eggs (average weight 60 grams). And don't forget to buy free range, because chickens deserve a bit of exercise too!

Sugar

Use caster sugar for best results. You can use coarser sugar but it takes longer for it to dissolve.
Liquid sugars like honey and golden syrup do not work. Soft brown sugar can be substituted entirely or partially for caster sugar to obtain a caramel-flavoured pav. Dark cane sugar and light muscovado sugar can be substituted for a quarter of the white sugar to achieve a malt flavour.

Acid

Without a small amount of acidic content, pavlova does not hold its shape. White vinegar is the staple ingredient, but it is not the only option. Lemon and lime juice work just as well although you need slightly more – 3 teaspoons juice substitutes for 2 teaspoons vinegar.
Other vinegars add different flavours too. Balsamic, white wine vinegar and red wine vinegar give a pav a very distinct wine flavour. However, avoid flavoured vinegars as you may not know exactly what is in them.

Cornflour

Cornflour only makes a difference in strengthening the structure of a pavlova when making a four or more egg white pavlova cake. It adds nothing to the recipe when baking miniatures, rolls and layer cakes – good news for those who cannot eat maize!

You can also make a cake without cornflour – it works fine though the result is a little different. With little or no air space created, the pavlova is flatter but just as tasty. It also has an indentation on top so it is a good idea to serve it with a tasty topping. Soft brown sugar pavlovas are best made without cornflour.

Whisking

If you have ever struggled with making pavlova, chances are the problem occurred during the whisking. Start by whipping the egg whites until they reach the stage of holding their shape when the beater passes through. Ideally, this is somewhere between soft and firm peak. This is the stage when it is possible to over-whip the whites. When this happens, the whites become grainy and begin to separate. Extra care should be taken especially when using an electric mixer.

For the highest-volume pavlova, I recommend the following technique using caster sugar:

Gradually add half the sugar for a cake (or all the sugar for a roll) while continuing to whip. Take about a minute – it doesn't need to be for any great length of time but adding sugar too fast will cause the mix to become watery. Continue to whip for around five minutes. If you are using an electric beater, the mix will thicken and gradually work its way up the blades as you whisk. When the mix is so stiff it pulls up between the beater blades and sits at the top of the whisks, you can stop. This is the perfect whisked state for a pavlova roll.

For a cake, fold through the remaining sugar, vinegar and cornflour. In my experience, this should give you a pavlova about 4 – 5 centimetres high with minimal sinking in the middle.

Whisking a pavlova for an extended period of time is a bit of a waste of time! If you instead focus on separating the sugar into halves and whisking in the first half until very firm, you will get a much better result.

Removing baking paper

A great cake can all go horribly wrong if the paper is not removed carefully. My best tip for removing the paper is to place the paper and pav onto the desired serving plate then fold the paper under the pav.

Placing the pav directly on top of where you want it to sit on the plate, roll away the paper underneath it. Let one side of the pav touch the plate at all times and keep your angle very slight so you are never actually lifting it off the plate.

A pavlova can buckle under its own weight so this technique will save it from breaking apart. It works whether the pav is warm or room temperature.

Presentation

Pavlova and whipped cream go together like, well . . . peaches and cream – but that doesn't mean it is the only option. Thick yoghurt makes a healthier substitute, and while it can be a little sour, a dash of vanilla will fix that. The filling in the Coconut Cream Layer Cake is also a winner with tropical toppings like passionfruit and mango.

I didn't want this book to be overly fruity so I have deliberately attempted to add in other flavourings like spices and chocolate which are accessible all year round. A word of warning, though – some ready-made sauces like passionfruit and raspberry are too strong for the humble pavlova, masking its delicate flavour. Fresh raspberries and passionfruit, on the other hand, work really well.

The only way to realise the ultimate pavlova experience for you personally is to have a go at a few of the recipes until you find your own preferences. It is my hope that readers will try my combinations and then create out of these their own favourites. I hope my book inspires you, your family and friends for years to come and keeps alive the time-honoured tradition of pavlova baking in our kitchens.

Genevieve Knights

Genevieve's must-try recipes from the book:
Lavender & Lemon Pavlova
Walnut Praline & Muscovado Pavlova

Wayne's must-try recipes from the book:
Coconut Cream Layer Cake
Danish Mallow Puffs

PAVLOVA CAKES

Classic Pavlova Cake

Cornflour isn't a necessary ingredient in pavlova and makes no difference as an addition to miniatures. However, adding cornflour to a pavlova cake does give you a higher result with a cake of around 3cm. For an extra-high cake (4–5cm high), try my technique – as specified in the "Pavlova Secrets" chapter – of whipping in half the sugar then folding through the remainder with the cornflour and vinegar.

4 egg whites
240g caster sugar
2 teaspoons white vinegar
2 teaspoons cornflour

Preheat the oven to 150°C fan setting. Draw a circle 20cm in diameter with a ballpoint pen onto a sheet of non-stick baking paper and set aside. In a large clean bowl, whip the egg whites until they form peaks. While continuing to whip, gradually rain in the 240g caster sugar. Then whip a further 8–10 minutes until all the sugar granules have dissolved.

Add the white vinegar and cornflour then fold in with a metal spoon very gently until combined. Pour the meringue into the centre of the penned ring. Using a spatula or palette knife, work the mix to the edges of the ring to create an even, flat disc. Hold the paper very taut and place onto a baking sheet. Place in the centre of the oven and bake for 15 minutes. Turn the heat down to 120°C and bake a further 35–40 minutes. Remove from the oven and leave to cool to room temperature. Serve with soft whipped cream and fresh fruit.

Serves 6

Walnut Praline & Muscovado Pavlova

The combination of muscovado sugar and toffee makes this dessert a bitter-sweet symphony of flavours and textures. Working with toffee is a little dangerous so always have ice water on hand. If the toffee touches any part of your skin, place in the water immediately.

3 egg whites
135g caster sugar
45g light muscovado sugar
1 ½ teaspoons white wine vinegar
1 ½ teaspoons cornflour
1 tablespoon strong liquid black coffee

additional 125g caster sugar
2 tablespoons water
70g chopped walnuts
300mls cream
additional 35g caster sugar
squeeze-bottle chocolate sauce

Preheat the oven to 150°C fan setting. Draw a circle 20cm in diameter with a ballpoint pen onto a sheet of non-stick baking paper and set aside. In a large clean bowl, whip the egg whites until they form peaks. While continuing to whip, gradually rain in the 135g caster and 45g muscovado sugar. Then whip a further 8–10 minutes until all the sugar granules have dissolved.

Add the vinegar, cornflour and coffee then fold in with a metal spoon very gently until combined. Pour the meringue into the centre of the penned ring. Using a spatula or palette knife, work the mix to the edges of the ring to create an even, flat disc. Hold the paper very taut and place onto a baking sheet. Place in the centre of the oven and bake for 10 minutes. Turn the heat down to 120°C and bake a further 35 minutes. Remove from the oven and leave to cool to room temperature.

Meanwhile, place the 125g caster sugar and water into a small pot. Stir to combine. Place on a medium heat and bring to the boil. Simmer until the caramel turns light brown then remove from the heat. Place a sheet of baking paper onto a chopping board and sprinkle over the walnuts. Drizzle over the toffee then leave to set for at least 10 minutes.

To serve, whip the cream and 35g caster sugar until soft whipped. Remove the pavlova from the paper and place on a serving plate. Smooth cream over the cake. Place shards of toffee and nuts onto the cake. Finish with drizzles of chocolate sauce. Serve immediately.

Serves 6

Lavender & Lemon Pavlova

Be sure to use English lavender (*Lavandula angustifolia*) for this recipe, as other lavender species are inedible. Lavender flavour in pavlova is gorgeously subtle and matches perfectly with fresh lemon. The ideal grand finale for a girls' night in or birthday cake for mum, serve it accompanied with chilled blanc de blanc bubbles or champagne.

4 egg whites
120g caster sugar
additional 120g caster sugar
zest of 1 lemon
3 teaspoons lemon juice
2 teaspoons cornflour

4 small English lavender buds, stalks removed
    and chopped very fine
400mls cream
200g mascarpone
additional 50g caster sugar
extra lavender petals for garnish

Preheat the oven to 150°C fan setting. Draw a circle 20cm in diameter with a ballpoint pen onto a sheet of non-stick baking paper and set aside. In a large clean bowl, whip the egg whites until they form peaks. While continuing to whip, gradually rain in the 120g caster sugar. Then whip a further 5 minutes until the meringue becomes very stiff.

Add the remaining 120g sugar, zest, lemon juice, cornflour and chopped lavender then fold in with a metal spoon very gently until combined. Pour the meringue into the centre of the penned ring. Using a spatula or palette knife, work the mix to the edges of the ring to create an even, flat disc. Hold the paper very taut and place onto a baking sheet.

Place in the centre of the oven and bake for 15 minutes. Turn the heat down to 120°C and bake a further 35 minutes. Remove from the oven and leave to cool to room temperature. Remove from the paper and place on a serving plate. Whip the cream, mascarpone and 50g sugar together until soft whipped. Smooth cream over the cake then rough up the surface a little. Top with extra lavender petals. Chill until serving time.

Serves 6–8

Turkish Pavlova

There is a common misconception that good volume in pavlova is connected with whisking in all the sugar until well dissolved. This is unfortunately not true. And, to prove the myth wrong, try this high-volume pavlova with half of the sugar folded in. The fact is, adding the first half of the sugar initially – yet still gradually – and whipping until very stiff, yields the most volume whether you whisk or fold in the remaining sugar.

4 egg whites
120g caster sugar
additional 120g caster sugar
2 teaspoons white vinegar
2 teaspoons cornflour
1 pinch ground cinnamon

1 pinch ground cardamom
300mls cream
50g runny honey
2 teaspoons rose water
70g toasted pistachios
10 pieces Turkish Delight, sliced in half

Preheat the oven to 150°C fan setting. Draw a circle 20cm in diameter with a ballpoint pen onto a sheet of non-stick baking paper and set aside. In a large clean bowl, whip the egg whites until they form peaks. While continuing to whip, gradually rain in the 120g caster sugar. Then whip a further 5 minutes until the meringue becomes very stiff.

Add the remaining 120g caster sugar, white vinegar, cornflour and spices then fold in with a metal spoon very gently until combined. Pour the meringue into the centre of the penned ring. Using a spatula or palette knife, work the mix to the edges of the ring to create an even, flat disc. Hold the paper very taut and place onto a baking sheet.

Place in the centre of the oven and bake for 15 minutes. Turn the heat down to 120°C and bake a further 35–40 minutes. Remove from the oven and leave to cool to room temperature. Remove from the paper and place on a serving plate. Whip the cream, honey and rose water together until soft whipped. Smooth cream over the cake. Top with the pistachios and Turkish Delight. Chill until serving time.

Serves 6–8

Coconut Cream Layer Cake

This gorgeous layer cake is relatively simple to make, but mind you take a little extra care when handling the layers as pavlova is delicate in texture and can crumble.

4 egg whites
240g caster sugar
2 teaspoons white vinegar
60g shredded coconut
additional shredded coconut for sprinkling
250mls cream
125g mascarpone
125g coconut cream
additional 50g caster sugar

Preheat the oven to 150°C fan setting. Draw 2 x 20cm in diameter circles with a ballpoint pen onto 2 sheets of non-stick baking paper and set aside. In a large clean bowl, whip the egg whites until they form peaks. While continuing to whip, gradually rain in the 240g caster sugar. Then whip a further 8–10 minutes until all the sugar granules have dissolved.

Add the white vinegar and 60g shredded coconut then fold in with a metal spoon very gently until combined. Divide the meringue between the penned rings. Using a spatula or palette knife, work the mix to the edges of the rings to create even, flat discs. Sprinkle the shredded coconut evenly over both layers. Holding the paper very taut, place the layers onto baking sheets. Place the baking sheets in the oven and bake for 5 minutes. Turn the heat down to 100°C and cook a further 30 minutes. Remove from the oven and leave to cool to room temperature.

Place the cream, mascarpone, coconut cream and additional 50g caster sugar into a medium-sized bowl. Beat with an electric beater until it is firm whipped. Remove the paper from the first cake layer and place upside down on a serving plate. Pile on the whipped cream and smooth over evenly leaving a centimetre gap at the edge. Remove the paper from the second cake layer and place on top. Chill until serving time.

Serves 6

Green Tea Pavlova

Green tea might be a surprising way to flavour a pavlova but the subtle flavours of the tea and pavlova complement each other nicely. Matched with an orange fruit like apricots or mandarins it is even better. If you don't have a pestle and mortar you can use a coffee grinder or chop the tea with a large sharp knife.

1 quality Japanese green tea bag
4 egg whites
240g caster sugar
2 teaspoons white vinegar
350mls cream
additional 50g caster sugar
orange fruit like orange, mandarin, or either fresh or poached apricots

Break the tea bag into a pestle and mortar. Crush the tea until powdered then set aside. Preheat the oven to 150°C fan setting. Draw a circle 20cm in diameter with a ballpoint pen onto a sheet of non-stick baking paper and set aside. In a large clean bowl, whip the egg whites until they form peaks. While continuing to whip, gradually rain in the 240g caster sugar. Then whip a further 8–10 minutes until all the sugar granules have dissolved.

Add the white vinegar and green tea reserving a pinch of tea for garnish. Fold in with a metal spoon very gently until combined. Pour the meringue into the centre of the penned ring. Using a spatula or palette knife, work the mix to the edges of the ring to create an even, flat disc. Hold the paper very taut and place onto a baking sheet.

Place in the centre of the oven and bake for 15 minutes. Turn the heat down to 120°C and bake a further 40–45 minutes. Remove from the oven and leave to cool to room temperature. Remove from the paper and place on a serving platter. In a medium-sized mixing bowl, whip the cream and additional 50g caster sugar until soft whipped. Smooth the cream over the pavlova and top with remaining powdered tea and fruit.

Serves 6

Lemon Curd Pavlova

Any extra liquid in a pavlova – like a third teaspoon of lemon juice – makes a slightly flatter pav with air space that can collapse in on itself. I have designed this recipe to use the indentation with a filling of curd topped with a little whipped cream and gorgeous lemon-coloured rose petals.

4 egg whites	120g butter
240g caster sugar	additional 120mls freshly squeezed lemon juice
3 teaspoons lemon juice	additional 120g caster sugar
2 teaspoons cornflour	200mls cream
zest of 2 lemons, separated	additional 1 teaspoon caster sugar
8 egg yolks	1 yellow rose

Preheat the oven to 150°C fan setting. Draw a circle 20cm in diameter with a ballpoint pen onto a sheet of non-stick baking paper and set aside. In a large clean bowl, whip the egg whites until they form peaks. While continuing to whip, gradually rain in the 240g caster sugar. Then whip a further 8–10 minutes until all the sugar granules have dissolved.

Add the 3 teaspoons lemon juice, cornflour and zest of 1 lemon then fold in with a metal spoon very gently until combined. Pour the meringue into the centre of the penned ring. Using a spatula or palette knife, work the mix to the edges of the ring to create an even, flat disc. Hold the paper very taut and place onto a baking sheet. Place in the centre of the oven and bake for 15 minutes. Turn the heat down to 120°C and bake a further 35–40 minutes. Remove from the oven and leave to cool to room temperature.

Meanwhile, place the egg yolks, butter, 120mls lemon juice, 120g caster sugar and remaining zest into a medium-sized pot. Stir continuously on a medium heat until it thickens which is just below simmering point. Don't allow it to boil as it will curdle. Leave to cool to room temperature.
Remove the paper and place the pav on a serving plate. Pour over the lemon curd and spread to the edges. Whip the cream and teaspoon caster sugar until soft whipped. Pour into the centre of the pav and spread out a little over the curd. Top with yellow rose petals. Serve immediately.

Serves 6

Mocha & Macadamia Pavlova

This recipe is a pavlova with a difference. The sugary nut topping gives it a delicious crunch and slightly caramel flavour that complements the mocha combination of coffee and chocolate. It's the perfect way to finish a midwinter meal by the fireside.

4 egg whites
120g caster sugar
additional 120g caster sugar
2 teaspoons white vinegar
2 teaspoons cornflour
2 teaspoons strong liquid black coffee
1 teaspoon cocoa
70g shelled macadamia nuts
1 tablespoon demerara sugar

Preheat the oven to 150°C fan setting. Draw a circle 20cm in diameter with a ballpoint pen onto a sheet of non-stick baking paper and set aside. In a large clean bowl, whip the egg whites until they form peaks. While continuing to whip, gradually rain in the 120g caster sugar. Then whip a further 5 minutes until the meringue becomes very stiff.

Add the remaining 120g caster sugar, white vinegar, cornflour and coffee then fold in with a metal spoon very gently until combined. Pour the meringue into the centre of the penned ring. Using a spatula or palette knife, work the mix to the edges of the ring to create an even, flat disc. Sift over the cocoa evenly. Sprinkle over the macadamias followed by the demerara sugar. Hold the paper very taut and place onto a baking sheet.

Place in the centre of the oven and bake for 15 minutes. Turn the heat down to 120°C and bake a further 35 minutes. Remove from the oven and leave to cool to room temperature. Remove from the paper and place on a serving plate. Serve with soft whipped cream on the side.

Serves 6

Saffron & Orange Pavlova

Powdered saffron does not require prior soaking to release its flavour and colour. If you can only source stamens, heat the vinegar with 2 teaspoons of boiling water until it steams. Sprinkle over the stamens and leave to stand for at least 20 minutes or overnight if possible. Add at the same time as the cornflour and orange zest.

4 egg whites

240g caster sugar

2 teaspoons white vinegar

large pinch of saffron powder

2 teaspoons cornflour

zest of half an orange

400mls cream

50g honey

60mls Cointreau or orange liqueur

1 orange, skin and white pith removed and discarded

extra saffron powder for garnish

Preheat the oven to 150°C fan setting. Draw a circle 20cm in diameter with a ballpoint pen onto a sheet of non-stick baking paper and set aside. In a large clean bowl, whip the egg whites until they form peaks. While continuing to whip, gradually rain in the 240g caster sugar. Then whip a further 8–10 minutes until all the sugar granules have dissolved. Add the white vinegar, saffron, cornflour and orange zest then fold in with a metal spoon very gently until combined.

Pour the meringue into the centre of the penned circle. Using a spatula or palette knife, work the mix to the edges of the ring to create an even, flat disc. Hold the paper very taut and place onto a baking sheet. Place in the centre of the oven and bake for 15 minutes. Turn the heat down to 120°C and bake a further 35–40 minutes. Remove from the oven and leave to cool to room temperature.

Place the cream, honey and Cointreau into a medium-sized bowl. Beat with an electric beater until soft whipped. Remove the pavlova from the paper and place on a large serving plate. Smooth over the cream evenly then rough it up a little. Top with slices of orange and a sprinkle of saffron.

Serves 6

Almond & Honey Layer Cake

Almonds, cream and honey are a simple yet beautiful flavour combination that works well with pavlova. Serve up this decadent cake for special occasions when you require a dramatic dessert to impress guests.

4 egg whites
240g caster sugar
2 teaspoons white vinegar
70g flaked almonds
300mls cream
50mls runny honey

Preheat the oven to 150°C fan setting. Draw 2 x 20cm in diameter circles with a ballpoint pen onto 2 sheets of non-stick baking paper and set aside. In a large clean bowl, whip the egg whites until they form peaks. While continuing to whip, gradually rain in the 240g sugar. Then whip a further 8–10 minutes until all the sugar granules have dissolved.

Add the white vinegar then fold in with a metal spoon very gently until combined. Divide the meringue between the penned rings. Using a spatula or palette knife, work the mix to the edges of the rings to create even, flat discs. Sprinkle the flaked almonds evenly over both layers. Holding the paper very taut, place the layers onto baking sheets. Place the baking sheets in the oven and bake for 5 minutes. Turn the heat down to 100°C and cook a further 30 minutes. Remove from the oven and leave to cool to room temperature.

Place the cream and honey into a medium-sized bowl then beat until soft whipped. Remove paper and place the first cake layer, nuts side up, on a serving plate. Pile on the cream and smooth over evenly leaving a centimetre gap at the edge. Remove the paper and top with the final cake layer. Chill until serving time.

Serves 6

After-dinner Mint Slab

We are used to having a chocolate mint with coffee after dinner and that is why this pavlova with the same flavourings doesn't leave you with a hankering to enrich it with cream. The shape also helps keep the pav very moist and marshmallow-like in the middle. It's the perfect lightweight way to end a rich meal.

4 egg whites
240g caster sugar
2 teaspoons white vinegar
2 teaspoons cornflour
¼ teaspoon edible peppermint essence
150g dark chocolate

Preheat the oven to 150°C fan setting. In a large clean bowl, whip the egg whites until they form peaks. While continuing to whip, gradually rain in the 240g caster sugar. Then whip a further 8–10 minutes until all the sugar granules have dissolved.

Add the white vinegar, cornflour and peppermint then fold in with a metal spoon very gently until combined. Draw a rectangle 12cm x 30cm in diameter with a ballpoint pen onto a sheet of non-stick baking paper. Pour the meringue into the centre of the penned rectangle. Using a spatula or palette knife, work the mix to the edges of the pen marks to create an even, flat rectangle. Hold the paper very taut and place onto a baking sheet.

Place in the centre of the oven and bake for 15 minutes. Turn the heat down to 120°C and bake a further 35–40 minutes. Remove from the oven and leave to cool to room temperature. Melt the chocolate in a bain marie or microwave. Spoon and swirl the chocolate onto the pav leaving it rough and rustic-looking. Chill for half an hour in the fridge. Remove from the paper and place onto a serving tray. Cut slices across the width and serve as an accompaniment to coffee.

Serves 6

Brown Sugar & Lime Pavlova

A brown-sugar pavlova is the same colour on the inside as the crust on the outside. It oozes gorgeous caramel flavour; and though it does have a slight indent on top, the dent is useful for holding a topping of whipped cream.

4 egg whites
240g soft brown sugar
3 teaspoons lime juice
350mls cream
additional 30g soft brown sugar
zest of one lime

Preheat the oven to 150°C fan setting. Draw a circle 20cm in diameter with a ballpoint pen onto a sheet of non-stick baking paper and set aside. In a large clean bowl, whip the egg whites until they form peaks. While continuing to whip, gradually rain in the 240g soft brown sugar. Then whip a further 8–10 minutes until all the sugar granules have dissolved.

Add the lime juice then fold in with a metal spoon very gently until combined. Pour the meringue into the centre of the penned ring. Using a spatula or palette knife, work the mix to the edges of the ring to create an even, flat disc. Hold the paper very taut and place onto a baking sheet. Place in the centre of the oven and bake for 15 minutes. Turn the heat down to 120°C and bake a further 35–40 minutes. Remove from the oven and leave to cool to room temperature.

To serve, remove paper and transfer the pavlova to a serving plate. Whip the cream and additional 30g soft brown sugar until soft whipped. Pour cream onto the pavlova and smooth over to cover the cake. Grate over fresh lime zest. Chill until serving time.

Serves 6

Greek Yoghurt, Fig & Honey Pavlova

Thin pavlovas take less time to cook than a pavlova cake and are reasonably easy to move around once free of their paper. They make an easy substitute for a tart base and can be served with cream or custard and topped with gorgeous, bright-coloured seasonal fruits.

3 egg whites
180g caster sugar
1 ½ teaspoons white vinegar
250g thick Greek yoghurt
¼ teaspoon vanilla paste or the scraped centre of a vanilla pod
30mls runny honey
8–9 fresh, red-centred figs
additional honey for drizzling

Preheat the oven to 150°C fan setting. Draw a 25cm x 30cm rectangle in ballpoint pen in the centre of a sheet of non-stick baking paper and set aside. In a large clean bowl, whip the egg whites until they form peaks. While continuing to whip, gradually rain in the 180g caster sugar. Then whip a further 8–10 minutes until all the sugar granules have dissolved.

Add the white vinegar then fold in with a metal spoon very gently until combined. Place a quarter of the mix into a piping bag fitted with a large plain nozzle. Pipe a border just inside the rectangle. Pipe the rest of the mix into the centre and add all the remaining meringue. With a palette knife, smooth the mix evenly to the edges of the piped border to create a flat rectangle. Hold the paper very taut and place onto a baking sheet. Place in the oven for 5 minutes. Turn the heat down to 100°C and cook a further 30 minutes. Remove from the oven and leave to cool to room temperature.

To serve, remove the pavlova from its paper and place on a rectangular platter. Mix the yoghurt, vanilla and 30mls honey until combined. Place dollops of the yoghurt evenly on top of the pavlova. Slice each fig in half and place attractively on top. Drizzle with a little extra honey. Serve immediately.

Serves 6

Banoffi Pavlova

Banoffi is the nickname for the fabulous paired flavours of banana and toffee. Matched up with a gorgeous brown-sugar pavlova base, the combination produces a truly-to-die-for dessert.

3 egg whites
180g soft brown sugar
1 ½ teaspoons white vinegar
250mls cream
additional 30g soft brown sugar
2 bananas
squeeze-bottle caramel sauce

Preheat the oven to 150°C fan setting. Draw a circle 20cm in diameter with a ballpoint pen onto a sheet of non-stick baking paper and set aside. In a large clean bowl, whip the egg whites until they form peaks. While continuing to whip, gradually rain in the 180g soft brown sugar. Then whip a further 8–10 minutes until all the sugar granules have dissolved.

Add the vinegar then fold in with a metal spoon very gently until combined. Pour the meringue into the centre of the penned ring. Using a spatula or palette knife, work the mix to the edges of the ring to create an even, flat disc. Hold the paper very taut and place onto a baking sheet. Place in the centre of the oven and bake for 10 minutes. Turn the heat down to 100°C and bake a further 30 minutes. Remove from the oven and leave to cool to room temperature.

To serve, remove the paper and transfer the pavlova to a serving plate. Whip the cream and additional 30g soft brown sugar until soft whipped. Pour cream onto the pavlova and smooth over to cover the cake. Peel and slice the bananas. Place slices attractively on top of the cream. Drizzle all over with caramel sauce. Serve immediately.

Serves 6

Tiramilova

Two classic dishes – tiramisu and pavlova – are combined to create this very yummy layer cake. Ironically, both desserts are named after women, tiramisu apparently being the maiden name of a confectioner's apprentice in the restaurant where the recipe is said to have originated. I made it once as a bit of a joke for friends, but it turned out so damn well that it has put in a number of appearances at my dinner parties!

6 egg whites
360g caster sugar
3 teaspoons white vinegar
1 tablespoon cocoa

250g mascarpone
5 tablespoons Kahlua
400mls cream
100g chocolate chips

Preheat the oven to 150°C fan setting. Draw 3 x 20cm in diameter circles with a ballpoint pen onto 3 sheets of non-stick baking paper. In a large clean bowl, whip the egg whites until they form peaks. While continuing to whip, gradually rain in the 360g caster sugar. Then whip a further 8–10 minutes until all the sugar granules have dissolved.

Add the white vinegar then fold in with a metal spoon very gently until combined. Divide the meringue between the penned rings. Using a spatula or palette knife, work the mix to the edges of the rings to create even, flat discs. Sift the cocoa evenly over all three layers. Holding the paper very taut, place the layers onto baking sheets. Place the baking sheets in the oven and bake for 5 minutes. Turn the heat down to 100°C and cook a further 30 minutes. Remove from the oven and leave to cool to room temperature.

Place the mascarpone and Kahlua into a medium-sized mixing bowl. Whisk together with an electric beater to combine. Add the cream and beat until firm whipped. Removing the paper from the layers as you go, place the first cake layer upside down on a serving plate. Pile on half the cream and smooth over evenly leaving a centimetre gap at the edge. Sprinkle over half the chocolate chips. Repeat the process with the second layer. Top with the final cake layer cocoa side up. Chill until serving time.

Serves 10

Triple Chocolate Pavlova

Your imagination is the limit for this dish as you can garnish with anything chocolaty that you fancy. Try toppings like gorgeous chocolate truffles, chocolate-coated nuts and raisins or chopped chocolate bars, especially those with gooey caramel.

4 egg whites
240g caster sugar
2 teaspoons white vinegar
2 teaspoons cornflour
2 teaspoons cocoa
additional 1 teaspoon cocoa

350mls cream
50g soft brown sugar
white and dark chocolate garnishes like
    shavings or truffles
squeeze-bottle chocolate sauce

Preheat the oven to 150°C fan setting. Draw a circle 20cm in diameter with a ballpoint pen onto a sheet of non-stick baking paper and set aside. In a large clean bowl, whip the egg whites until they form peaks. While continuing to whip, gradually rain in the 240g caster sugar. Then whip a further 8–10 minutes until all the sugar granules have dissolved.

Add the white vinegar, cornflour and 2 teaspoons sifted cocoa then fold in with a metal spoon very gently until combined. Pour the meringue into the centre of the penned ring. Using a spatula or palette knife, work the mix to the edges of the ring to create an even, flat disc. Sift over the remaining 1 teaspoon cocoa. Hold the paper very taut and place onto a baking sheet.

Place in the centre of the oven and bake for 15 minutes. Turn the heat down to 120°C and bake a further 35–45 minutes. Remove from the oven and leave to cool to room temperature. Remove from the paper and place on a serving plate. Whip the cream and soft brown sugar until soft whipped. Smooth the cream over the pavlova. Top with chocolate garnishes. Chill until serving time then, when ready to serve, drizzle with chocolate sauce.

Serves 6

MINIATURE PAVLOVAS

Classic Miniature Pavlovas

Essentially the same recipe as the classic pavlova cake, the baking time and cooking temperatures are different when making smaller pavlovas. You can use this recipe as a guide to create a miniature version of the pavlova cake flavours in this cookbook. Remember, though, to substitute 3 teaspoons lemon or lime juice for 2 teaspoons vinegar if required.

4 egg whites
240g caster sugar
2 teaspoons white vinegar
soft whipped cream
kiwi berries (pictured) or kiwifruit

Preheat the oven to 150°C fan setting. Line a tray with non-stick baking paper then set aside. In a large clean bowl, whip the egg whites until they form peaks. While continuing to whip, gradually rain in the 240g caster sugar. Then whip a further 8–10 minutes until all the sugar granules have dissolved.

Add the white vinegar then fold in with a metal spoon very gently until combined.
Using 2 dessertspoons, place 12 large spoonfuls of pavlova mix onto the baking tray. Place in the oven for 5 minutes. Turn the heat down to 100°C and cook a further 30 minutes. Remove from the oven and leave to cool to room temperature. Serve 1 or 2 per person, topped with soft whipped cream and sliced kiwi berries or kiwifruit.

Serves 6

Chocolate Dusted Puffs

This is the kind of recipe I come up with when I don't want to go shopping and instead make myself cook from the larder. They are often the tastiest recipes! These puffs are delicious and look so pretty. Serve them with soft whipped cream on the side and let your family and guests help themselves.

4 egg whites
240g caster sugar
2 teaspoons white vinegar
2 tablespoons cocoa

Preheat the oven to 150°C fan setting. Line a tray with non-stick baking paper then set aside. In a large clean bowl, whip the egg whites until they form peaks. While continuing to whip, gradually rain in the 240g caster sugar. Then whip a further 8–10 minutes until all the sugar granules have dissolved.

Add the white vinegar then fold in with a metal spoon very gently until combined. Sift the cocoa over whipped whites. Without stirring, place spoonfuls of pavlova mix onto the baking tray. Place in the oven for 5 minutes. Turn the heat down to 100°C and cook a further 30 minutes. Remove from the oven and leave to cool to room temperature.

Serves 6

Peppermint Candy Kisses

Peppermint candy kisses can colour your tongue pink, making them perfect for kids' parties. They are also very appropriate to serve at Christmas time thanks to the peppermint candy cane.

2 egg whites
120g caster sugar
1 teaspoon white vinegar
¼ teaspoon edible peppermint essence
¼ teaspoon red food colouring
150mls cream

Preheat the oven to 150°C fan setting. Line a tray with non-stick baking paper then set aside. In a large clean bowl, whip the egg whites until they form peaks. While continuing to whip, gradually rain in the 120g caster sugar. Then whip a further 8–10 minutes until all the sugar granules have dissolved.

Add the white vinegar and peppermint essence then fold in with a metal spoon very gently until combined. Prepare a piping bag with a large fluted nozzle. Drizzle the food colouring evenly over the whipped whites. Without stirring, spoon the mix into the piping bag. Pipe teaspoon-sized kisses onto the prepared tray. Place in the oven for 5 minutes. Turn the heat down to 100°C and cook a further 30 minutes. Remove from the oven and leave to cool. When ready to serve, whip the cream. Sandwich together 2 kisses of a similar size with a little cream. Serve immediately.

Makes 15 kisses

Chocolate-dipped Coconut Bites

These after-dinner treats are quick and easy to make. Get the kids to help with the chocolate dipping – and don't forget to clean your fingers each time they touch chocolate to avoid visible chocolate fingerprints.

2 egg whites
120g caster sugar
1 teaspoon white vinegar
50g desiccated coconut
200g milk chocolate

Preheat the oven to 150°C fan setting. Line a tray with non-stick baking paper then set aside. In a large clean bowl, whip the egg whites until they form peaks. While continuing to whip, gradually rain in the 120g caster sugar. Then whip a further 8–10 minutes until all the sugar granules have dissolved.

Add the white vinegar and coconut then fold in with a metal spoon very gently until combined. Prepare a piping bag with a large plain nozzle. Spoon the mix into the piping bag. Pipe teaspoon-sized lots of the mix in the shape of Hershey's Kisses onto the prepared tray. Place in the oven for 5 minutes. Turn the heat down to 100°C and cook a further 30 minutes. Remove from the oven and leave to cool.

Place a sheet of non-stick baking paper onto a fresh tray. Melt the chocolate in a bain marie or microwave. While holding the tips, dip the bottom half of the pavlova bites into the chocolate. Shake off any excess chocolate then place onto the paper. Chill until set – about 45 minutes. Best served on the day they are made.

Makes 20

Piped Raspberry, Passionfruit & Crème Fraîche Nests

For a change from whipped cream try this luscious crème fraîche topping. Its slight tartness pairs beautifully with fresh berries and the sweetness of pavlova.

3 egg whites
180g caster sugar
1 ½ teaspoons white vinegar
150g crème fraîche
150g thick plain yoghurt
additional 60g caster sugar
fresh raspberries
2 fresh passionfruit

Preheat the oven to 150°C fan setting. Line a tray with non-stick baking paper then set aside. In a large clean bowl, whip the egg whites until they form peaks. While continuing to whip, gradually rain in the 180g caster sugar. Then whip a further 8–10 minutes until all the sugar granules have dissolved.

Add the white vinegar then fold in with a metal spoon very gently until combined. Fit a piping bag with a large plain nozzle. Fill the bag and pipe 6 nests onto the baking tray. Start by piping in a spiral circle 6cm in diameter. Then pipe a circle of meringue on top of the bases around the edge.

Place in the oven for 5 minutes. Turn the heat down to 100°C and cook a further 35 minutes. Remove from the oven and leave to cool to room temperature. To serve, mix together crème fraîche, yoghurt and 60g caster sugar. Place the nests onto individual plates. Top with the crème fraîche mix, fresh raspberries and passionfruit. Serve immediately.

Serves 6

Chocolate Hedgehogs

Here is another simple idea for a kids' party. Chocolate Hedgehogs are yummy and lots of fun to make. Don't be afraid to hand the brush to the kids and get them to paint the hedgehogs in chocolate. A good tip is to leave them on the bench during brushing, rather than holding them, to avoid crumbling.

2 egg whites
120g caster sugar
1 teaspoon white vinegar
100g dark chocolate
25g white chocolate

Preheat the oven to 150°C fan setting. Line a tray with non-stick baking paper then set aside. In a large clean bowl, whip the egg whites until they form peaks. While continuing to whip, gradually rain in the 120g caster sugar. Then whip a further 8–10 minutes until all the sugar granules have dissolved.

Add the white vinegar then fold in with a metal spoon very gently until combined. Place the mix into a piping bag with a large fluted nozzle. Pipe tablespoon amounts on an angle onto the tray then pull away the nozzle to create a pointed nose for the hedgehogs. Place in the oven for 5 minutes. Turn the heat down to 100°C and cook a further 30 minutes. Remove from the oven and leave to cool to room temperature.

Melt the dark chocolate in a bain marie or microwave. Brush some chocolate onto each hedgehog, avoiding its "face". Pipe dark chocolate circles for its eyes. Refrigerate until set. Melt the white chocolate and pipe into the centre of each eye. Finish the eyes with a small dot of piped dark chocolate. Leave to set.

Makes 20

Brown Sugar & Lemon Pavlovas

You can substitute the white vinegar in a basic pavlova recipe with lemon juice. When zest is added as well, the flavour is of pure, fresh, zingy lemon!

4 egg whites
120g soft brown sugar
120g caster sugar
zest of one lemon
3 teaspoons lemon juice
150mls cream
additional 30g soft brown sugar
extra soft brown sugar for garnish

Preheat the oven to 150°C fan setting. Line a tray with non-stick baking paper then set aside. In a large clean bowl, whip the egg whites until they form peaks. While continuing to whip, gradually rain in the 120g soft brown sugar and 120g caster sugar. Then whip a further 8–10 minutes until all the sugar granules have dissolved.

Add the lemon zest and juice then fold in with a metal spoon very gently until combined. Using 2 dessertspoons, place 12 large spoonfuls of pavlova mix onto the baking tray. Place in the oven for 5 minutes. Turn the heat down to 100°C and cook a further 30 minutes. Remove from the oven and leave to cool to room temperature. To serve, place 2 pavlovas per person on serving plates. Whip the cream and 30g soft brown sugar. Top each pavlova with a dollop of soft whipped cream and a sprinkle of soft brown sugar. Serve immediately.

Serves 6

Saffron Kisses

Saffron is one of the few spices that translates equally well into savoury and sweet dishes. You will love its unique flavour in these yummy sweet kisses. Serve them for morning and afternoon tea or as part of a high tea.

2 teaspoons boiling water
2 teaspoons white vinegar
1 large pinch saffron stamens
2 egg whites
240g caster sugar
150mls cream

Pour the boiling water and vinegar over the saffron. Heat the liquid in a microwave until steaming. Leave to soak for at least 2 hours or overnight if possible. Preheat the oven to 150°C fan setting. Line a tray with non-stick baking paper then set aside.

In a large clean bowl, whip the egg whites until they form peaks. While continuing to whip, gradually rain in the 240g caster sugar. Then whip a further 8–10 minutes until all the sugar granules have dissolved. Add the saffron vinegar then fold in with a metal spoon very gently until combined.

Prepare a piping bag with a large fluted nozzle. Spoon the mix into the piping bag. Pipe teaspoon-sized kisses onto the prepared tray. Place in the oven for 5 minutes. Turn the heat down to 100°C then cook a further 30 minutes. Remove from the oven and leave to cool. When ready to serve, whip the cream. Sandwich together 2 kisses of a similar size with a little cream. Serve immediately.

Makes 15 kisses

Balsamic Strawberry Pavlovas

Balsamic vinegar and strawberries are an unusual but fantastic dessert combination. A small amount of black pepper also adds a refreshing spikiness. They are a perfect match with rosé champagne or sparkling wine.

4 egg whites
120g caster sugar
120g soft brown sugar
2 teaspoons quality balsamic vinegar
additional teaspoon quality balsamic vinegar
20 hulled strawberries
milled black pepper
soft whipped cream

Preheat the oven to 150°C fan setting. Line a tray with non-stick baking paper then set aside. In a large clean bowl, whip the egg whites until they form peaks. While continuing to whip, gradually rain in the 120g caster sugar and 120g brown sugar. Then whip a further 8–10 minutes until all the sugar granules have dissolved.

Add the balsamic vinegar then fold in with a metal spoon very gently until combined.
Using dessertspoons place 12 large spoonfuls of pavlova mix onto the baking tray. Place in the oven for 5 minutes. Turn the heat down to 100°C and cook a further 30 minutes. Remove from the oven and leave to cool to room temperature.

Slice the strawberries into thin rounds. Toss in the additional teaspoon of balsamic vinegar. Add a good grind of black pepper and marinate for at least 10 minutes. Serve the pavlovas topped with soft whipped cream and the strawberry slices.

Serves 6

Piped Marshmallow & Raspberry Pavlovas

An elegant alternative to pavlova cake are beautiful piped pavlovas topped with your favourite fruits or sweets. If you are handy with a piping bag, give these a go next time you have guests. They are much easier to serve than a regular pavlova and far softer to eat than meringues. They work really well for kids' parties too and can double as a birthday cake with a lit candle in each one.

4 egg whites
240g caster sugar
2 teaspoons white vinegar
250mls cream, soft whipped
fresh raspberries
2 handfuls of mini marshmallows

Preheat the oven to 150°C fan setting. Line a tray with non-stick baking paper then set aside. In a large clean bowl, whip the egg whites until they form peaks. While continuing to whip, gradually rain in the 240g caster sugar. Then whip a further 8-10 minutes until all the sugar granules have dissolved.

Add the white vinegar then fold in with a metal spoon very gently until combined. Fit a piping bag with a medium-sized fluted nozzle. Fill the bag and pipe 16 nests onto the baking tray. Start by piping in a spiral circle 4cm in diameter. Then pipe a circle of meringue on top of the base at the edge. Continue piping 4 layers high to create a hollow nest.

Place in the oven for 5 minutes. Turn the heat down to 100°C and cook a further 45 minutes. Remove from the oven and leave to cool to room temperature. Fill a clean piping bag with soft whipped cream and pipe into the centres of each nest. Top with fresh raspberries and mini marshmallows. Arrange into a circle on a cake stand. Serve immediately.

Serves 8

Rose & Vanilla Pavlovas

You can make an instant vanilla sugar by blending a chopped vanilla pod with 250g caster sugar then sifting it to remove the pod. The best way though, is to use your scraped pods from previous recipes. Place them in a jar with caster sugar and let sit indefinitely.

4 egg whites
240g vanilla sugar
2 teaspoons white vinegar
150mls cream
additional 2 teaspoons vanilla sugar
½ teaspoon rose water
different-coloured rose petals for garnish

Preheat the oven to 150°C fan setting. Line a tray with non-stick baking paper then set aside. In a large clean bowl, whip the egg whites until they form peaks. While continuing to whip, gradually rain in the 240g vanilla sugar. Then whip a further 8–10 minutes until all the sugar granules have dissolved.

Add the white vinegar then fold in with a metal spoon very gently until combined. Divide the mix into 6 dollops on the baking tray. Shape into 8cm discs with a palette knife or spatula (the same shape as a pavlova cake). Place in the oven for 5 minutes. Turn the heat down to 100°C and cook a further 35 minutes. Remove from the oven and leave to cool to room temperature.

To serve, whip the cream with the 2 teaspoons vanilla sugar and rose water. Place the pavs onto 6 serving plates and top with whipped cream. Garnish with rose petals and serve immediately.

Serves 6

PAVLOVA ROLLS

Jelly Tip Pavlova Roll

The flavour combination of raspberry, cream and chocolate was immortalised in the iconic Jelly Tip ice cream produced by food manufacturer Tip Top in the 1950s. The name refers to ice cream on a stick with a raspberry jelly tip, coated in chocolate. Though this iconic combination of flavours has morphed over the years into everything from cocktails to cheesecakes, if a Kiwi tastes it, they will always smile nostalgically and proudly announce: "Jelly Tip"!

4 egg whites
125g caster sugar
2 teaspoons white vinegar
½ an 85g packet raspberry jelly crystals
80mls cream
150g dark chocolate
additional 200mls cream
additional 25g caster sugar

Preheat the oven to 160°C fan setting. Line a tray with non-stick baking paper then set aside. In a large clean bowl, whip the egg whites until they form peaks. While continuing to whip, gradually rain in the 125g caster sugar. Then whip a further 5 minutes until all the sugar granules have dissolved.

Add the white vinegar and jelly crystals then fold in with a metal spoon very gently until combined. With a spatula, smooth the mix onto the prepared tray in the shape of a rectangle 25cm x 30cm. Bake for 8 minutes. Remove from the oven and leave to cool for 10 minutes.

Meanwhile, place the 80mls cream into a medium-sized pot. Bring to a simmer then add the chocolate. Stir to combine then briefly whisk until smooth and set aside. Whip the 200mls cream and 25g caster sugar until soft whipped. Smooth evenly over the roll. Roll up widthways, pulling away the paper underneath as you go. Place onto a fresh piece of baking paper and brush chocolate all over. Place in the fridge for at least 30 minutes. Keep chilled until serving time.

Serves 6

Fresh Coconut & Marshmallow Pavlova

It occurred to me when I pulled this pav from the oven – why do we roll up pavlova rolls? Sometimes they can look so beautiful just as they are! This pav uses grated fresh coconut underneath it, so it won't stick to your plate. If fresh coconut is not available, substitute it with shredded dried coconut.

1 fresh coconut
4 egg whites
120g caster sugar
2 teaspoons white vinegar
150mls cream
50mls coconut cream
50g soft brown sugar

Crack the coconut in half with a hammer. With a small sharp knife eke off the edible flesh and discard the hard husk. With a peeler, shave some of the white flesh across the edge so each shaving has a brown strip on one side. Place the shavings into cool water. Grate 50g of remaining coconut and set aside.

Preheat the oven to 160°C fan setting. Brush or spray a baking tray with a little water then line with non-stick baking paper. Set the tray aside. In a large clean bowl, whip the egg whites until they form peaks. While continuing to whip, gradually rain in the 120g caster sugar. Then whip a further 5 minutes until all the sugar granules have dissolved.

Add the white vinegar then fold in with a metal spoon very gently until combined. With a spatula, smooth the mix onto the prepared tray in the shape of a rectangle 25cm x 30cm. Sprinkle evenly with the grated coconut. Bake for 8 minutes. Remove from the oven and leave to cool for 10 minutes. To serve, turn out the pavlova upside down onto a serving platter. Peel off the paper. Whip the cream, coconut cream and 50g soft brown sugar together until soft whipped. Smooth the cream over the pavlova in an even layer. Sprinkle over the coconut shavings. Chill until serving time.

Serves 6

Cookies & Cream Pavlova Roll

The surface of a pav roll has a natural stickiness and I think it's fun to find something to stick to it! I love the effect cocoa has, making the surface look cracked and gorgeous in all its rustic, chocolaty-coloured glory.

4 egg whites
120g caster sugar
2 teaspoons white vinegar
1 tablespoon cocoa
150g chocolate chip cookies
200mls cream

Preheat the oven to 160°C fan setting. Line a tray with non-stick baking paper then set aside. In a large clean bowl, whip the egg whites until they form peaks. While continuing to whip, gradually rain in the 120g caster sugar. Then whip a further 5 minutes until all the sugar granules have dissolved.

Add the white vinegar then fold in with a metal spoon very gently until combined. With a spatula, smooth the mix onto the prepared tray in the shape of a rectangle 25cm x 30cm. Dust evenly with the cocoa. Bake for 8 minutes. Remove from the oven and leave to cool for 10 minutes.

Place the cookies in a food processor and blend until they reach the consistency of fine breadcrumbs. Whip the cream to a soft-whipped stage. Fold the biscuit crumbs into the cream. Place clean baking paper on top of the pavlova and turn upside down. Peel off the top layer of paper. Smooth the cream evenly over the pavlova rectangle. Roll up widthways firmly. Keep chilled until serving time.

Serves 6

Passionfruit & Mascarpone Pavlova Roll

My favourite pavlova topping as a child was fresh passionfruit pulp and soft whipped cream, always just in time for my autumn birthday! Here is a contemporary take on the old favourite using a marshmallow-like roll and mascarpone for extra stability and creamy flavour.

4 egg whites
120g caster sugar
2 teaspoons white vinegar
200g mascarpone
100g passionfruit
200mls cream
additional 50g caster sugar

Preheat the oven to 160°C fan setting. Line a tray with non-stick baking paper then set aside. In a large clean bowl, whip the egg whites until they form peaks. While continuing to whip, gradually rain in the 120g caster sugar. Then whip a further 5 minutes until all the sugar granules have dissolved.

Add the white vinegar then fold in with a metal spoon very gently until combined. With a spatula, smooth the mix onto the prepared tray in the shape of a rectangle 25cm x 30cm. Bake for 8 minutes. Remove from the oven and leave to cool for 10 minutes.

Whisk together the mascarpone, passionfruit, cream and 50g caster sugar until firm enough to hold its shape when the beater passes through the mix. Smooth the mix evenly over the pavlova rectangle. Roll up widthways, pulling away the paper underneath as you go. Transfer to a serving dish. Keep chilled until serving time.

Serves 6

Pistachio & Chocolate Pavlova Roll

When filled with chocolate and stored overnight, pavlova rolls lose some of their aeration. This is not a bad thing! Rolled with pistachio nuts, this roll turns into a slightly chewy, chocolate and nut confectionery similar to nougat.

4 egg whites
125g caster sugar
2 teaspoons white vinegar
80mls cream
150g milk chocolate
70g pistachios, toasted and chopped fine

Preheat the oven to 160°C fan setting. Line a tray with non-stick baking paper then set aside. In a large clean bowl, whip the egg whites until they form peaks. While continuing to whip, gradually rain in the 125g caster sugar. Then whip a further 5 minutes until all the sugar granules have dissolved.

Add the white vinegar then fold in with a metal spoon very gently until combined. With a spatula, smooth the mix onto the prepared tray in the shape of a rectangle 25cm x 30cm. Bake for 8 minutes. Remove from the oven and leave to cool for 10 minutes.

Melt the cream and chocolate together in a bain marie or microwave then stir until smooth in consistency. Brush the chocolate all over the pavlova rectangle. Sprinkle over evenly a third of the pistachios. Chill for 15 minutes to firm up the chocolate. Roll up widthways, pulling away the paper underneath as you go. Remove the paper and smother with the remaining pistachios. Place onto a fresh piece of baking paper and roll up tightly. Chill overnight. Slice into 12 pieces to serve.

Serves 6

Brown Sugar & Cinnamon Pavlova Roll

If you have never made a pavlova roll before, this simple recipe might be the best place to start. Take your time adding the sugar, about a minute, then continue to whip until the egg white becomes very thick and sits at the top of the whisks – around 5 more minutes. Whipping the whites this thick yields a pavlova roll with the best volume.

4 egg whites
120g soft brown sugar
2 teaspoons white vinegar
200mls cream
30g caster sugar
⅛ teaspoon ground cinnamon

Preheat the oven to 160°C fan setting. Line a tray with non-stick baking paper then set aside. In a large clean bowl, whip the egg whites until they form peaks. While continuing to whip, gradually rain in the 120g soft brown sugar. Then whip a further 5 minutes until all the sugar granules have dissolved.

Add the white vinegar then fold in with a metal spoon very gently until combined. With a spatula, smooth the mix onto the prepared tray in the shape of a rectangle 25cm x 30cm. Bake for 8 minutes. Remove from the oven and leave to cool for 10 minutes.

Whip the cream, caster sugar and cinnamon together. Smooth the cream evenly over the cooled pavlova. Roll up widthways, pulling away the paper underneath as you go. Place on a serving platter and chill until serving time.

Serves 6

Fairy Pavlova Roll

I always loved eating fairy bread as a child and it inspired me to make this dish. Fairy bread is simply white buttered bread sprinkled with hundreds and thousands. I thought I could do a bit better than that for the kids so I rolled into the pavlova an easy and delicious strawberry mousse.

4 egg whites
120g caster sugar
2 teaspoons white vinegar
3 teaspoons gelatine powder
3 tablespoons boiling water
250g fresh or thawed frozen strawberries (at room temperature)
additional 50g caster sugar
250mls cream
hundreds and thousands for sprinkling

Preheat the oven to 160°C fan setting. Line a tray with non-stick baking paper then set aside. In a large clean bowl, whip the egg whites until they form peaks. While continuing to whip, gradually rain in the 120g caster sugar. Then whip a further 5 minutes until all the sugar granules have dissolved.

Add the white vinegar then fold in with a metal spoon very gently until combined. With a spatula, smooth the mix onto the prepared tray in the shape of a rectangle 25cm x 30cm. Bake for 8 minutes. Remove from the oven and leave to cool for 10 minutes.

Stir the gelatine powder into the boiling water until dissolved. Purée the strawberries and additional 50g caster sugar until smooth. Pulse in the gelatine. Separately whisk the cream until it forms soft peaks. With a hand whisk, whisk the strawberry purée into the cream until combined. Place the pavlova onto a firm tray that fits in the fridge. Smooth over the mousse evenly. Chill until semi-set – about 20 minutes. Roll up widthways, pulling away the paper underneath as you go. Sprinkle well with hundreds and thousands. Keep chilled until serving time.

Serves 10 kids

Lamington Pavlova Roll

For this recipe I have combined two Australian inventions, pavlova roll and lamingtons. The combination makes a decadent and tasty dessert the whole family will enjoy on special occasions or for a weekday treat.

4 egg whites
125g caster sugar
2 teaspoons white vinegar
80mls cream
additional 25g caster sugar
150g dark chocolate
250mls cream
additional 25g caster sugar
½ cup shredded or desiccated coconut

Preheat the oven to 160°C fan setting. Line a tray with non-stick baking paper then set aside. In a large clean bowl, whip the egg whites until they form peaks. While continuing to whip, gradually rain in the 125g caster sugar. Then whip a further 5 minutes until all the sugar granules have dissolved.

Add the white vinegar then fold in with a metal spoon very gently until combined. With a spatula, smooth the mix onto the prepared tray in the shape of a rectangle 25cm x 30cm. Bake for 8 minutes. Remove from the oven and leave to cool for 10 minutes.

Meanwhile, place the 80mls cream and 25g caster sugar into a medium-sized pot. Bring to a simmer then add the chocolate. Stir to combine then briefly whisk until smooth and set aside. Whip the 250mls cream and 25g caster sugar until soft whipped. Smooth cream evenly over the roll. Roll up widthways, pulling away the paper underneath as you go.

Brush a light coat of chocolate all over the roll. Sprinkle over two thirds of the coconut. Place upside down onto a fresh piece of baking paper. Brush the underside with the remaining chocolate and sprinkle with remaining coconut. Place in the fridge for 30 minutes to set and keep chilled until serving time.

Serves 6

Red Berry Pavlova Roll

You can use a combination of fresh or frozen mixed berries for this recipe or feature a favourite berry like boysenberry or raspberry. Blueberries are not quite juicy enough to work on their own but make a nice addition to a berry mix.

350g mixed fresh or frozen berries
50g caster sugar
60mls water
3 tablespoons cornflour
additional 3 tablespoons cool water
4 egg whites
additional 120g caster sugar
2 teaspoons white vinegar

Place the berries, 50g caster sugar and 60mls water into a medium-sized pot. Bring to a simmer then remove from the heat. Stir together the cornflour and 3 tablespoons water. Slowly add cornflour mix to the pot while stirring. Return to the heat and bring to a simmer while constantly stirring.
When simmering and thick, remove from the heat and leave to cool.

Preheat the oven to 160°C fan setting. Line a tray with non-stick baking paper then set aside. In a large clean bowl, whip the egg whites until they form peaks. While continuing to whip, gradually rain in the 120g caster sugar. Then whip a further 5 minutes until all the sugar granules have dissolved.
Add the white vinegar then fold in with a metal spoon very gently until combined. With a spatula, smooth the mix onto the prepared tray in the shape of a rectangle 25cm x 30cm. Bake for 8 minutes. Remove from the oven and leave to cool for 10 minutes.

To serve, smooth the berry mix evenly over the pavlova rectangle. Roll up lengthways, pulling away the paper underneath as you go. Place onto a serving platter. Chill until serving time.

Serves 6

Rocky Road Slice

This is a quick and easy dessert for a girls' night in or a treat for the whole family. It takes very little time to prepare, looks amazing and tastes even better.

4 egg whites
120g caster sugar
2 teaspoons white vinegar
2 teaspoons cocoa
28 marshmallows
150g milk chocolate

Preheat the oven to 160°C fan setting. Line a tray with non-stick baking paper then set aside. In a large clean bowl, whip the egg whites until they form peaks. While continuing to whip, gradually rain in the 120g caster sugar. Then whip a further 5 minutes until all the sugar granules have dissolved.

Add the white vinegar then fold in with a metal spoon very gently until combined. With a spatula, smooth the mix onto the prepared tray in the shape of a rectangle 15cm x 22cm. Evenly sift over the cocoa. Bake for 8 minutes. Remove from the oven and leave to cool for 10 minutes.

Remove from the paper and place on a serving platter. Place on the marshmallows in even rows of 4 across the width. Melt the chocolate in a bain marie or microwave and stir until smooth. Drizzle over all the chocolate. Chill until set – around 20 minutes. To serve, cut slices across the width.

Serves 6

Orange Curd Pavlova Roll

You can make orange dust by peeling the skin from oranges, removing any white pith and simmering in a 50/50 white sugar and water syrup for 15 minutes. Drain the skins then bake spread out on baking paper at 180°C for 15 minutes. Blend the dried skins in a coffee grinder until powdered and store in an airtight container. Orange dust has a long shelf life and also tastes great as an ice-cream topping.

6 egg yolks
90g butter
120g caster sugar
90mls freshly squeezed orange juice
zest of 1 orange
300g cream cheese
4 egg whites
additional 120g caster sugar
2 teaspoons white vinegar

Place the egg yolks, butter, 120g caster sugar, orange juice and zest into a medium-sized pot. Stir continuously on a medium heat until just below boiling point. Don't allow it to boil as it will curdle. Cool and then blend on a high speed with the cream cheese. Chill for 2 hours before filling the roll.

Preheat the oven to 160°C fan setting. Line a tray with non-stick baking paper then set aside. In a large clean bowl, whip the egg whites until they form peaks. While continuing to whip, gradually rain in 120g caster sugar. Then whip a further 5 minutes until all the sugar granules have dissolved.

Add the white vinegar then fold in with a metal spoon very gently until combined. With a spatula, smooth the mix onto the prepared tray in the shape of a rectangle 25cm x 30cm. Bake for 8 minutes. Remove from the oven and leave to cool for 10 minutes.

Smooth the curd evenly over the pavlova rectangle. Roll up lengthways, pulling away the paper underneath as you go. Place onto a fresh piece of baking paper and sprinkle well with orange dust. Chill until serving time.

Serves 6

INNOVATIVE PAVLOVA

Strawberry Syrup Marshmallow Cake

The versatility of the Australian Pavlova Roll recipe re-emerges here in the form of a gorgeous cake. I am officially in love with this recipe now and still can't quite work out why it was smoothed into a large rectangle and rolled up when it makes such a wonderful dessert in the same shape as the original pavlova.

100g caster sugar
50mls water
10 fresh strawberries, hulled and chopped
4 egg whites
additional 120g caster sugar
2 teaspoons white vinegar
a small handful of toasted pistachios

Place the 100g caster sugar, water and strawberries into a medium-sized pot and bring to a boil. Simmer on a low heat for 2 minutes then remove from the heat and leave to cool.

Preheat the oven to 160°C fan setting. Draw a circle 20cm in diameter with a ballpoint pen onto a sheet of non-stick baking paper and set aside. In a large clean bowl, whip the egg whites until they form peaks. While continuing to whip, gradually rain in the 120g caster sugar. Then whip a further 5 minutes until all the sugar granules have dissolved.

Add the white vinegar then fold in with a metal spoon very gently until combined. Pour the meringue into the centre of the penned ring. Using a spatula or palette knife, work the mix to the edges of the ring to create an even, flat disc. Hold the paper very taut and place onto a baking sheet. Bake for 10 minutes. Remove from the oven and leave to cool for 10 minutes.

To serve, roll the paper away from under the pavlova while edging it onto a shallow serving plate. Pour the cooled syrup over the cake, along with some of the poached strawberries.
Sprinkle with pistachios.

Serves 6

Danish Mallow Puffs (Flødeboller)

Not technically pavlova, flødeboller is a Danish chocolate-coated marshmallow cookie. I have included it because the technique in making the marshmallow centre isn't the typical whipped gelatine, egg whites and sugar recipe but instead closer to pavlova roll – minus the vinegar – and baked for a short amount of time. I also included them because they are so very yummy!

150g plain flour
75g cold butter, sliced into small cubes
50g caster sugar
3 egg yolks
cool water

3 egg whites
additional 120g caster sugar
250g milk chocolate
1 tablespoon Trex

Preheat the oven to 200°C and line a baking tray with non-stick baking paper. Place the flour in a medium-sized mixing bowl and rub in the butter until it resembles fine breadcrumbs. Stir in the 50g caster sugar. Add the yolks and stir with a fork to combine. Stir in enough water to form dough, being careful not to overwork. Dust work bench with a little flour and roll out to a thickness of a quarter centimetre. Cut 15 x 4cm circles with a plain round cookie cutter. Place on the tray. Bake for 8–10 minutes in the oven until lightly golden. Remove from the oven and leave to cool to room temperature.

In a large clean bowl, whip the egg whites until they form peaks. While continuing to whip, gradually rain in the 120g caster sugar. Then whip a further 5 minutes until all the sugar granules have dissolved. Prepare a piping bag with a large plain nozzle. Spoon the meringue into the piping bag. Pipe the mix onto the biscuit bases in a spiral to create meringue towers around 6cm high. Place in the oven for 3–4 minutes until the meringue has puffed and browned slightly. Remove from the oven and leave to cool.

Place a sheet of non-stick baking paper onto a tray. Melt the chocolate and Trex in a bain marie or microwave. While holding the base, dip the meringue into the chocolate and turn until completely covered. Shake off any excess mixture then place onto the paper. Chill until set – about an hour.

Makes 15

Nougat Parfait

Parfait is an ice cream that is aerated by whipped cream rather than churning. This means you can add delicate ingredients that would normally be crushed in the churning process. Pavlova is a great example of such an ingredient and changes from crunchy fluff to marshmallow as it freezes.

170g dried cranberries or craisins
8 egg yolks
60g runny honey
60g caster sugar
500mls cream
½ teaspoon vanilla bean paste or 1 scraped vanilla bean
70g pistachios
70g flaked almonds
100g crumbled pavlova

Line a large ceramic dish with baking paper leaving plenty of excess paper on 2 opposite sides. Set the dish aside. Place the cranberries in a small bowl and cover with boiling water. Leave to soak for 15 minutes. Drain well. Place the egg yolks, honey and sugar into a large-sized mixing bowl. Whip with an electric beater for 5–6 minutes until very thick and pale yellow in colour. In a fresh bowl, whip up the cream and vanilla until soft whipped.

Add the drained cranberries, pistachios, flaked almonds and crumbled pavlova to the yolks. Fold through with a metal spoon. Lastly, fold in the whipped cream. Pour into the prepared dish, cover with cling film and freeze. To serve, unwrap and pull on the paper to release the parfait from the dish. Turn upside down onto a chilled serving platter. Cut into slices and serve immediately.

Serves 10

Raspberry Lamington Pavlova Cake

This cake is a little fiddly but well worth the extra effort. Raspberry lamingtons are a well-loved down under icon and the original pavlova roll recipe creates a moist, light and airy lamington layer cake.

85g packet raspberry jelly crystals
250mls boiling water
4 egg whites
120g caster sugar
2 teaspoons white vinegar

shredded coconut for sprinkling
400mls cream
½ teaspoon vanilla bean paste or 1 scraped
   vanilla bean
additional 50g caster sugar

Stir together the jelly crystals and water until dissolved then set aside to cool. Preheat the oven to 160°C fan setting. Draw 2 x 20cm in diameter circles with a ballpoint pen onto 2 sheets of non-stick baking paper then set aside. In a large clean bowl, whip the egg whites until they form peaks.
While continuing to whip, gradually rain in the 120g caster sugar. Then whip a further 5 minutes until all the sugar granules have dissolved.

Add the white vinegar then fold in with a metal spoon very gently until combined. Divide the meringue between the penned rings. Using a spatula or palette knife, work the mix to the edges of the rings to create even, flat discs. Holding the paper very taut, place the layers onto baking sheets. Place the baking sheets in the oven and bake for 8 minutes. Remove from the oven and leave to cool to room temperature.

When the jelly is thick and almost set, brush each cake layer with the jelly. Chill the cakes for 15 minutes or until set then repeat the process 2 more times. You can briefly reheat the jelly if it starts to turn lumpy. When the last coat of jelly is on the cake layers, sprinkle each well with shredded coconut.
Chill for at least 2 hours.

Place the cream, vanilla and additional 50g caster sugar into a medium-sized bowl. Beat with an electric beater until soft whipped. Place the first cake layer jelly side up on a serving plate. Pile on the whipped cream and smooth over evenly leaving a centimetre gap at the edge. Top with the final cake layer, jelly side up. Chill until serving time.

Serves 6

Rose-scented Eton Mess

Eton Mess is a dish that originated in England. Legend has it that the boys from Eton College loved to break up the components from their desserts into a mess before consuming them. Or it could be a way to use up leftover pavlova or meringue. Either way, it's very easy and to-die-for tasty.

250g fresh strawberries, hulled
½ teaspoon rose water
1 tablespoon caster sugar
250mls cream
½ teaspoon vanilla bean paste or 1 scraped vanilla bean
1 cup crumbled pavlova
1 handful of dried rose petals

Slice the strawberries into quarters and place in a medium-sized mixing bowl. Add the rose water and sugar then toss together. Leave to marinate for 10 minutes to release the strawberry juices. Whip the cream and vanilla until thick but not whipped. Sprinkle over the crumbled pavlova and dried rose petals. Strain off the red juice from the strawberries and reserve it. Add the strawberries to the bowl.

Give the bowl one stir with a wooden spoon. The idea is that you can still see the individual components instead of covering them with cream. Spoon into 6 serving bowls. Drizzle over the strawberry juice. Serve immediately.

Serves 6

Port-soaked Prune & Chocolate Eton Mess

This time instead of a fresh fruit approach, I have opted for one of my favourite dessert flavour combinations. Port, prunes and chocolate make a scrumptious combo for a more adult take on the classic Eton Mess.

20 pitted prunes
90mls port
1 tablespoon caster sugar
250mls cream
½ teaspoon vanilla bean paste or 1 scraped vanilla bean
1 cup crumbled pavlova
squeeze-bottle chocolate sauce

Slice the prunes into halves and place in a medium-sized mixing bowl. Add the port and caster sugar then toss together. Leave to marinate for at least 10 minutes or for 2 hours if possible. Whip the cream and vanilla until thick but not whipped. Sprinkle over the crumbled pavlova. Strain off the port from the prunes and reserve it. Add the prunes to the bowl. Squeeze over some chocolate sauce.

Give the bowl one stir with a wooden spoon. The idea is that you can still see the individual components instead of covering them with cream. Spoon into 6 serving bowls. Drizzle over the reserved port. Serve immediately.

Serves 6

Toffee & Lemon Marshmallow Cake

If you are flicking through the pages of this book looking for a recipe that is super yum, low in fat, takes about 17 minutes to cook from scratch – and the ingredients are already in your kitchen – you just found it!

4 egg whites	additional 120g caster sugar
120g caster sugar	50mls water
2 teaspoons white vinegar	50mls fresh lemon juice
zest of 2 lemons separated	additional 25mls water

Preheat the oven to 160°C fan setting. Draw a circle 20cm in diameter with a ballpoint pen onto a sheet of non-stick baking paper and set aside. In a large clean bowl, whip the egg whites until they form peaks. While continuing to whip, gradually rain in the 120g caster sugar. Then whip a further 5 minutes until all the sugar granules have dissolved.

Add the white vinegar and zest of 1 lemon then fold in with a metal spoon very gently until combined. Pour the meringue into the centre of the penned ring. Using a spatula or palette knife, work the mix to the edges of the ring to create an even, flat disc. Bake for 10 minutes. Remove from the oven and leave to cool to room temperature.

While the cake is cooking, place the additional 120g caster sugar and 50mls water into a medium-sized pot then stir to combine. Bring to the boil then turn the heat down to medium. Simmer until the sugar starts to turn golden brown. Standing well clear to avoid splatters, add the lemon juice, remaining lemon zest and 25mls water. Stir with a wooden spoon to combine. Simmer while stirring until you have a smooth, lump-free syrup then remove from the heat.

To serve, roll the paper away from under the pavlova while edging it onto a shallow serving plate. Pour the cooled syrup over the cake.

Serves 6

Rhubarb & Pavlova Fool

Use a homemade or bought pavlova for this recipe. You could even use leftover cream-covered pavlova pressed into the base of the glass. It's a great way to create a fresh dessert for 6 out of leftovers from the previous night's pudding!

50g caster sugar
250mls water
200g rhubarb
1 cup crumbled pavlova
1 ½ cups cream
½ cup crème fraîche
¼ cup runny honey

Place the caster sugar and water in a medium-sized pot and bring to a simmer. Meanwhile, remove any rough ends from the rhubarb. Slice rhubarb into 5cm-long lengths. Add the rhubarb to the water and simmer for 5 minutes. Remove from the heat and leave to cool. Purée in a food processor then set aside.

Distribute the crumbled pavlova evenly between 6 serving glasses. Separately whip the cream, crème fraîche and honey until it forms firm peaks. Pour the rhubarb purée over the cream but do not stir it. Spoon the rhubarb sauce and cream into the serving glasses to create a rippled fruit fool. Serve immediately.

Serves 6

Boysenberry Ice-cream Cake

Pavlova cake layers are almost exactly the same at room temperature as when frozen except that in the cold they become a little firmer. This makes them ideal for an ice-cream sandwich! Use any of your favourite flavoured ice creams for this recipe and don't forget that brown-sugar pavlova layers work extremely well with caramel and chocolate-flavoured ice creams.

4 egg whites
240g caster sugar
2 teaspoons white vinegar
1 litre boysenberry ripple ice cream

Preheat the oven to 150°C fan setting. Draw 2 x 20cm in diameter circles with a ballpoint pen onto 2 sheets of non-stick baking paper. In a large clean bowl, whip the egg whites until they form peaks. While continuing to whip, gradually rain in the 240g caster sugar. Then whip a further 8–10 minutes until all the sugar granules have dissolved.

Add the white vinegar then fold in with a metal spoon very gently until combined. Divide the meringue between the penned rings. Using a spatula or palette knife, work the mix to the edges of the rings to create even, flat discs. Holding the paper very taut, place the layers onto baking sheets. Place the baking sheets in the oven and bake for 5 minutes. Turn the heat down to 100°C and cook a further 30 minutes. Remove from the oven and leave to cool to room temperature.

Leave the ice cream to sit at room temperature for around 5 minutes. Remove the first cake layer from the paper and place on a serving plate. Place scoops of the ice cream evenly on top of the pavlova layer. Remove the second layer from its paper and place on top of the ice cream. Press down the layer gently to flatten the cake a little. Freeze until serving time.

Serves 6

Sherbet Cones

Here is a nostalgic look at a kids' treat from the seventies. We used to pay a small fortune for sherbet in little white bags with a straw out one side (considering what it cost to produce). Or you could buy its sophisticated marshmallow-in-a-cone cousin on a "rich" week! It was all about the fizzing sensation on the tongue that we loved. Be sure to serve these at your next kids' or seventies themed party.

½ teaspoon citric acid
1 teaspoon tartaric acid
¾ teaspoon baking soda
40g flavoured jelly crystals (raspberry pictured)
40g caster sugar
4 egg whites
additional 120g caster sugar
12 flat-based, coloured ice-cream cones

Preheat the oven to 160°C. Sieve the citric acid, tartaric acid and baking soda into a small-sized mixing bowl. Stir in the jelly crystals and 40g caster sugar then set aside.

In a large clean bowl, whip the egg whites until they form peaks. While continuing to whip, gradually rain in the 120g caster sugar. Then whip a further 5 minutes until all the sugar granules have dissolved. Prepare a piping bag with a large fluted or plain nozzle. Spoon the meringue into the piping bag. Pipe meringue into the ice-cream cones, filling the base, then pipe a spiral on top to create meringue towers around 4cm high. Place on a baking tray then very carefully place in the oven. Bake for 3 minutes until browned slightly. Remove from the oven and leave to cool to room temperature.

One at a time, hold each cone over the sherbet and spoon the sherbet all over the meringue to completely cover it. Be sure to fill any cracks where the meringue meets the cone.

Makes 12

Strawberry & Pavlova Trifle

If you don't have a strawberry liqueur, you can substitute with other liquors like brandy, sherry and whisky. Basically, any of the traditional trifle liquors will do and likewise the fruit can be substituted for whatever is tasty and in season.

1 punnet strawberries
2 tablespoons strawberry liqueur
250g bought vanilla custard
150–200g pavlova (bought or homemade)
100g chopped dark or milk chocolate

Slice the strawberries into thin rounds. Toss with the strawberry liqueur and leave to marinate for 10 minutes. Careful to keep the layers flat, spoon the strawberries with liqueur and custard into 4 serving glasses separating each layer with crumbled pavlova and chopped chocolate. Serve immediately.

Serves 4

Mandarin & Chocolate Marshmallow Cake

Every year during the mandarin season, it occurs to me how quick we are to throw away what must be kilos of skins. Like oranges, they store a concentrated flavour in the oil of their skins. To zest a mandarin use a microplane on a whole fruit and grate onto a board so the oils won't splatter and affect the egg white foam or surface chocolate. You can peel and eat the segments after the zest is removed as normal.

4 egg whites

120g caster sugar

2 teaspoons white vinegar

zest of 2 mandarins, separated

80mls cream

additional 25g caster sugar

80g butter

150g dark or milk chocolate

Preheat the oven to 160°C fan setting. Draw a circle 20cm in diameter with a ballpoint pen onto the sheet of non-stick baking paper and set aside. In a large clean bowl, whip the egg whites until they form peaks. While continuing to whip, gradually rain in the 120g caster sugar. Then whip a further 5 minutes until all the sugar granules have dissolved.

Add the white vinegar and zest of one mandarin then fold in with a metal spoon very gently until combined. Pour the meringue into the centre of the penned ring. Using a palette knife, work the mix to the edges of the ring to create an even, flat disc. Hold the paper very taut and place onto a baking sheet. Bake for 10 minutes. Remove from the oven and leave to cool for 10 minutes.

Meanwhile, place the cream, 25g caster sugar and butter into a medium-sized pot. Bring to a simmer then add the chocolate. Stir to combine then briefly whisk until smooth. Pour the chocolate directly onto the cake. Smooth chocolate onto and around the sides to give it an even coating all over. Remove excess chocolate from the base and chill for at least an hour.

To serve, run a knife around the base to separate the chocolate from the paper. Roll the paper away from under the pavlova while edging it onto a shallow serving plate. Top with the remaining mandarin zest.

Serves 6

Glossary

Bain marie
A double-pot water bath used for gentle heating or keeping food warm.

Baking soda
Leavening agent that can be used in a dough or batter containing an acidic ingredient. One of the components in baking powder.

Caster sugar
Fine white sugar.

Citric acid
Crystalline powder made from the skins of citrus fruit.

Coconut, desiccated
Fine-cut dried coconut.

Coconut, shredded
Coarse-cut dried coconut.

Cornflour
White starch powder made from corn kernels.

Craisins
Sweetened dried cranberries.

Crème fraîche
French for "fresh cream". Originally produced in Normandy, a European version of sour cream but with less acidity and lighter texture.

Demerara sugar
A variety of unrefined, granulated cane sugar.

Electric beater
Hand-held mixer with two whisks.

Electric mixer
A stand mixer with a large whisk and bowl.

Eton Mess
Dessert of crumbled pavlova (or meringue), fresh fruit and cream, stirred together.

Flaked almonds
Almonds with skin on shaved very thin.

Ganache
Chocolate, butter and cream melted together then chilled. Used as a base for chocolate truffles, cake glazes and piped cake garnishes.

Jelly Tip
A raspberry-tipped ice cream on a stick, covered in chocolate. The words "jelly tip" also refer to the flavour combination of raspberry, cream and chocolate.

Kiwi berries
A miniature version of kiwifruit with a soft, green, edible skin.

Mascarpone
An Italian method of making cream cheese that has a full-cream flavour and softer texture in comparison to cream cheese.

Meringue
White foam of whipped egg whites and sugar.

Meringues
Meringue that is shaped and oven-dried.

Mocha
A combination of coffee and chocolate flavours.

Muscovado sugar
An unrefined brown sugar with a strong molasses flavour.

Palette knife
A long thin paddle with a handle made of flexible metal used for shaping meringue.

Praline
A combination of toffee and nuts either ground fine or served in shards.

Rocky Road
A sweet made by mixing marshmallows and chocolate.

Rose water
Distilled water infused with rose extract.

Saffron
A precious yellow spice with a distinct yellow colour and flavour.

Tartaric acid
A natural fruit acid in the form of a fine white powder.

Tiramisu
A dessert made from sponge fingers or amoretti biscuits, mascarpone, chocolate and coffee.

Turkish Delight
Rose, lemon or mint flavoured confectionery made from starch and sugar.

Vanilla bean
The seed pod of a vanilla plant derived from orchids.

Vanilla paste
Paste made from vanilla seeds.

Zest
The grated skin of citrus fruit.

Index

Conversion Chart

Measuring

We use the following measures:
One metric measuring cup holds approximately 250ml; one metric tablespoon holds 15ml; one metric teaspoon holds 5ml.

The difference between one country's measuring cups and anothers is within a two or three teaspoon variance and will not affect your results.

All cup and spoon measurements are level. The most accurate way of measuring dry ingredients is to weigh them. When measuring liquids, use a clear glass or plastic jug with the metric markings.

We use large eggs with an average weight of 60g.

Dry Measures

METRIC	IMPERIAL
15g	½oz
30g	1oz
60g	2oz
90g	3oz
125g	4oz (¼lb)
155g	5oz
185g	6oz
220g	7oz
250g	8oz (½lb)
280g	9oz
315g	10oz
345g	11oz
375g	12oz (¾lb)
410g	13oz
440g	14oz
470g	15oz
500g	16oz (1lb)
750g	24oz (1½lb)

Liquid Measure

METRIC	IMPERIAL
30ml	1 fluid oz
60ml	2 fluid oz
100ml	3 fluid oz
125ml	4 fluid oz
150ml	5 fluid oz (¼ pint)
190ml	6 fluid oz
250ml	8 fluid oz
300ml	10 fluid oz (½ pint)
500ml	16 fluid oz
600ml	20 fluid oz (1 pint)
1000ml (1 litre)	1¾ pints

Length Measures

1cm	½in
2cm	¾in
2.5cm	1in
5cm	2in
6cm	2½in
8cm	3in
10cm	4in
13cm	5in
15cm	6in
18cm	7in
20cm	8in
23cm	9in
25cm	10in
28cm	11in
30cm	12in (1ft)

Oven Temperatures

These oven temperatures are only a guide for conventional ovens. For fan-forced ovens, check the manufacturer's manual.

	C (CELCIUS)	F (FARENHEIT)	GAS MARK
Very slow	120	250	½
Slow	150	275 – 300	1 – 2
Moderately slow	160	325	3
Moderate	180	350 – 370	4 – 5
Moderately hot	200	400	6
Hot	220	425 – 450	7 – 8
Very hot	240	475	9

pavlova

First edition published by White Knights Publishing 2010
This UK edition published in 2011 by Accent Press Ltd,
The Old School, Upper High Street, Bedlinog,
Mid-Glamorgan, CF46 6RY

Designed by Wayne Knights
Edited by Mike Wagg
Genevieve's portrait photographed by Anja Gallas

A very special thank you to Helen Leach for her assistance with
historical references.

Typeset by Milan Bishwakarma using IGP:Frontlist Interactive Publisher
www.infogridpacific.com

Printed and bound by Toppan Printing (SZ) Limited, China

The *pavlova* recipes were tested entirely with free-range eggs.

Cover photo – Classic Miniature Pavlova

ISBN 9781907016486

www.accentpress.co.uk
www.pavlovabook.com
www.genevievescuisine.com